Also available in this series from Quadrille:

MINDFULNESS   KINDNESS
QUIET   BRIDESMAIDS
FRIENDSHIP   PRIDE
LOVE   GRATITUDE
CONFIDENCE   POSITIVITY
TIDINESS   UNITY
HAPPINESS   HOPE
MOTHERHOOD   JOY
LUCK   COURAGE
US   MANIFESTING
SEX   SELF-LOVE
CHRISTMAS   EMPOWERMENT
SISTERHOOD   RESILIENCE
SELF-CARE

the little book of

FOCUS

Quadrille

Focus

Definition:

noun

1. A point of convergence or concentration; an object of sustained or intense interest or attention.

2. The sustained or intense concentration of interest and attention on a particular thing.

3. The ability to sustain such concentration.

Have you put this book down yet to pick up a device?

If so, stop.

Focus.

Keep reading.

Learn the art of sustaining focus on one thing at a time, allowing yourself to master your concentration and excel at the task in hand.

" There is no force equal to a woman determined to rise."

W.E.B. DU BOIS

Focus...otherwise known as...

Concentration

Engagement

Being engrossed

Fixation

Hard work

Paying attention

Zeroing in

Focus does NOT mean

Compulsion

Mania

Becoming plagued

Torment

Obsession

"Concentrate all your thoughts upon the work at hand. The sun's rays do not burn until brought to a focus."

ALEXANDER GRAHAM BELL

Concentration. Focus.
Mindfulness. Zen.

Such ideas hold hands together.
They seek to encourage that acute
sense of being fully alive within an
activity. Whatever the task, whoever
the people involved, wherever it takes
place, we are invited to be wholly
present in both mind and body.

" You will have power over your mind – not outside events. Realize this, and you will find strength."

MARCUS AURELIUS

Q: Is it true that humans now have an attention span shorter than that of a goldfish?

A: Sort of, depends who you ask.

Woah there – can this possibly be true? Studies are varied but Art Kramer, professor of psychology and director of the Center for Cognitive and Brain Health at Northeastern University suggests that the average time a human can focus on one thing has dropped from two and a half minutes to 45 seconds. For reference, a goldfish is said to have an attention span of nine seconds.

Is your focus orientated in the right direction? Do you look backwards to focus on what went wrong, or forwards to focus on how to put it right?

Why is focus important? I thought it was all about the vision.

True, the vision/goal/dream comes first. Second comes the plan: how do I get there? Third comes action. At the tail end of the journey comes FOCUS. For without it, the action falters and the whole vision disappears. Imagine focus as the fuel driving you to your dream destination.

Stoic philosopher Seneca wrote a brief tract called *On the Shortness of Life* – a two-thousand-year-old reminder to make the most of our brief time on Earth. He writes, "Most wretched is the condition of those who labour at engrossments [giving all your attention to something] that are not even their own, who regulate their sleep by that of another, their walk by the pace of another, who are under orders in case of the freest things in the world – loving and hating."

Questions prompted by Seneca's thoughts on attention:

1. How much of my focus is given to things others require of me?

2. Have I or someone else chosen that upon which I am focusing my attention?

3. Love and hate – have I chosen where I deploy these emotions or am I prompted by an outside force or person?

Q: What's the opposite of a focused individual?

A: Absent minded, thoughtless, flaky, inattentive, distracted.

Are we happy with such labels, do any of them apply to us? Can our lack of focus negatively affect others? If we find these descriptions uncomfortable, are we able to evaluate why?

" Knowing that conscious decisions and personal memory are much too small a place to live, every human being streams at night into the loving nowhere, or during the day, in some absorbing work."

RUMI

Try peppermint oil to aid focus

Nicholas Culpeper, the 17th-century herbalist, noted of peppermint that it was 'comfortable for the head and memory', and indeed a more recent study by Sage Journals suggests that peppermint improves clerical task performances including speedy and accurate typing.

Burning peppermint oil while working can provide associative sensory prompts: the aroma of peppermint reminds us that it is time to focus.

Questions to ask at the break of day:

Where shall I put my focus today?

On whom should I focus?

Where is my focus needed?

Focus like a feline

Watch a cat as it stalks in the long grass and you will see eyes opened with pupils narrowed, ears pointed forward, legs bent and body low to the ground, angled towards the focus of their attention.

As we begin a task that requires our full attention, can we be more feline? Is our body aligned? Are our eyes, our limbs, our minds all lasering in on the same locus? A cat could not catch a mouse if it was playing with a ball of string. Nor can we complete our task properly if also making a call or rooting around in the fridge for something to nibble.

Golden focus tip

Set a daily priority.

This can be very general, such as 'getting through the day' or as specific as 'planting out the sunflower seedlings'; as dreary as 'completing the remortgage', or as ambitious as 'beginning piano lessons'. The mere act of writing down that upon which you wish to focus will help clarify your intentions and give energy to your actions.

Morning mantras to summon a focused mind

I shall only attempt one task at a time.

My head is clear, my mind is focused.

I have the power to control and direct my attention.

Today I shall withstand distractions.

With each calm breath I take, I deepen my concentration.

How to maximize focus if you're a lark

You're up and zinging, ready to plunge into the day. These early hours are your best time to tackle those demanding tasks and work productively – what would take you two hours in the evening only takes an hour in the morning.

When preparing a lark's routine, remember:

1. **To hydrate** – perhaps not full caffeine just yet, instead try a hot water and lemon.

2. **To stretch** – a full wake-up routine is not needed, but a downward dog might be enough to tell your body there's work to be done.

3. **To feel the sun** – if not yet risen, at least open the curtains to feel the full benefits of the dawn.

Containing nearly a quadrillion synapses, your brain is the most complex object in the universe; there is nothing remotely comparable. Who, then, is in charge of it? A screen, a video game, a phone? How happy are we that this remarkable mass of 86 billion neurons is so easily distracted by kitten videos? Decide to reclaim your brain and put its wondrous powers to your service.

Our instinct tells us that being outside and feeling the sun on our skin helps us in all sorts of ways, so it's reassuring to see that a 2022 large-scale study in Finland has found a link between sun exposure and better cognitive function, improving things including visual memory, new learning, visual processing and sustained attention.

Sunlight encourages the release of beneficial hormones, neurotransmitters and brain molecules that support focus:

1. Dopamine – the vital neurotransmitter that supports memory, learning and attention.

2. Serotonin – the mood-boosting hormone that promotes focus and feelings of calm.

3. Brain-derived neurotrophic factor – a clever little molecule that's involved in processing, memory and feeling alert.

Let sunlight be your concentration elixir. Begin each day by basking in its warm embrace. Step outside, even for a few moments, and allow the sun's rays to kiss your skin. This simple act can awaken your senses, boost your mood and ignite your cognitive abilities. Incorporate sunlight into your routine by taking short walks during breaks, enjoying outdoor meals or simply sitting by a window. Remember, a little sunshine goes a long way in nourishing your body and mind's ability to focus.

Five-minute focus task

Drink your morning coffee outside. Not on the go. Not in the car. Not in bed. Take it outside and do nothing but drink your coffee and let the morning sun awaken your mind.

" *Now is the accepted time, not tomorrow, not some more convenient season. It is today that our best work can be done and not some future day or future year. It is today that we fit ourselves for the greater usefulness of tomorrow. Today is the seed time, now are the hours of work, and tomorrow comes the harvest and the playtime.*"

W.E.B. DU BOIS

" *There is a power under your control that is greater than poverty, greater than the lack of education, greater than all your fears and superstitions combined. It is the power to take possession of your own mind and direct it to whatever ends you may desire.*"

ANDREW CARNEGIE

Create zones of focus

WORK: Position your work desk so that it faces against a blank wall to avoid distractions.

INSPIRATION: For solitary moments of entertainment and daydreaming, style the terrace, balcony, bath or window seat as beautifully as possible.

RECHARGING: Please no, seriously... no screens in bedrooms.

Try not to muddle up these varying places of focus: keep laptops out of bed, glasses of wine away from the work desk, phones from the place of inspiration. By habituating ourselves to different mindsets in these various spaces we are better able to focus on either work, inspiration or sleep.

" *The giants of the race have been men of concentration, who have struck sledgehammer blows in one place until they have accomplished their purpose. The successful men of today are men of one overmastering idea, one unwavering aim, men of single and intense purpose.*"

ORISON SWETT MARDEN

Focus aid: go old school, use a pen and paper

It is impossible to think one thought while writing down another. The act of writing in black and white allows you to focus all your attention on one individual idea or issue at a time.

When there is too much to do, avoid prevarication and panic by reaching for old-fashioned pen and paper. Instead of risking distraction while using your phone to write notes or send an urgent message, manually write down the problems. The solutions will present themselves.

Stirring a ragu, overseeing homework, answering a work email – is it really possible to do all of these things well? Yes, if we harness the ability to transfer our focus from one task to another.

How to practise focus transference when multitasking

- Understand that although you are overseeing three or more tasks, it is only possible to give attention to each task separately.

- Make eye contact with whoever is requiring your attention.

- Give clear time boundaries: I will help you in one minute.

- Avoid bringing utensils or tech from one task to another.

- Change postures when focusing on different tasks, sitting beside the person needing assistance rather than hovering.

The easiest way to be more present with family members, friends and colleagues is to completely remove digital devices from interactions, allowing everyone to focus only on the present and each other. Shared faraday pouches or Yondr boxes, in which everyone can safely store their phones during mealtimes or meetings, are a fantastic way of reviving communal concentration.

Golden focus reminder

Never underestimate our ability to form our own characters. If we decide we want to become more focused, we can.

The fruit bowl. The fridge. Social media. The cookie jar. Snap.

It is no wonder we are all struggling to focus, when there are so many exciting distractions at our fingertips. When lengthy focus is required, it is imperative that we physically move ourselves away from delicious and digital distractions.

Create a sweet-shop digital prison

Invest in an old-school sweet-shop jar and fill with your favourite wrapped sweets (no-one wants the bonbon icing sugar infiltrating phones) and submerge whatever digital device you need to imprison. Once you've retrieved the device after a morning of laser-like focus, reward yourself with a toothsome treat.

Three ways to digitally imprison devices and increase focus

1. Hide your phone in your child's bedroom – the mortification that comes with realizing your self-control is no better than a child's helps to keep the phone hidden until you've finished concentrating on the task at hand.

2. Turn the phone off before closing the digital prison door. This extra step will help stop you opening the drawer to have a 'quick check'.

3. If self-control is rock bottom, ask your partner, colleague or flatmate to take care of your device for the period of time required.

Focus challenge: Time-train your focus

1. Set an old-school alarm clock for ten minutes (not your phone!).

2. Forbid yourself from doing anything other than the task at hand before the timer beeps.

3. Gradually increase the time to 20, 30, 40 minutes.

4. Before long, you will find yourself working in full flow for up to an hour at a time.

" Try to learn something about everything and everything about something."

THOMAS HUXLEY

Develop focus-centred habits

As creatures of habit, we all have a fantastic ability to form behaviours that support our wellbeing. We clean our teeth and moisturize our skin without thinking, so why not also zap our brain into focus mode?

1. Secure digital devices in your favourite safe place.

2. Spray peppermint oil.

3. Play your focus playlist.

4. FOCUS!

" First, forget inspiration. Habit is more dependable. Habit will sustain you whether you're inspired or not."

OCTAVIA E. BUTLER

Golden focus tip:

Set your mind to the solution rather than ruminating over the problem.

" The more I study, the more insatiable do I feel my genius for it to be."

ADA LOVELACE

" People sometimes attribute my success to my genius; all the genius I know anything about is hard work."

ALEXANDER HAMILTON

Ideas for discussion: is focus just
another word for hard work?

Create a concentration seesaw

For every moment of concentration, reward yourself with the same number of moments of pleasure.

Have you heard of the biophilia hypothesis? It's the notion that humans have a natural affinity with nature (*bios* means 'life' and *philia* means 'love of'). The colour green has long been associated with feelings of calm, which can aid concentration. Choose forest-inspired colour schemes around your home office.

Create a focus playlist

- **Discover low-fi music.** It's 'low-fidelity' and therefore contains imperfections and lower-quality sound recordings. The raw edge to the music helps the listener to tune out and focus on the job in hand.

- **Discover the Mozart Effect.** The breathtaking brilliance of Mozart, Bach or Beethoven, if played at a gentle volume, can stimulate the brain to greater focus and activity.

- **Avoid lyrics.** Words can suddenly attach themselves to your thoughts and distract you completely. For pure concentration, stick to harmonies alone.

- **Experiment with video game music.** Deliberately designed to lull gamers into hours of play, gaming music offers just the right amount of atmosphere for brain clarity.

- **Zone in on one track to kickstart your period of focus.** Let your brain know it's time to concentrate by playing the same track at the beginning of every period of intense work.

- **Create the playlist before you need to concentrate.** Ensure the albums or soundtracks are lined up to play for a good couple of hours and do not require you to flit to and from your work.

Discover the Pomodoro Technique

Invented by student Francesco Cirillo in the 1980s using nothing more than a tomato-shaped kitchen timer, this is a straightforward method of breaking up big tasks into manageable chunks.

1. Decide on your task.

2. Set the timer for 25 minutes, or whatever you can manage.

3. Work on the task for the set period.

4. Stop when the timer rings and take a short break, ideally 5–10 minutes, to allow yourself to absorb and understand the work.

5. Repeat from step two until you complete four sessions.

6. After four are completed, treat yourself to a long break, say 20 to 30 minutes.

7. Return to step two and repeat until the task is complete or begin another task.

" Force yourself to reflect on what you read, paragraph by paragraph."

SAMUEL TAYLOR COLERIDGE

Indulge in greenery-based micro-breaks to rev up concentration

An Australian study found that briefly viewing a green roof improved students' cognitive performance. Students were invited to complete demanding computer tasks and then asked to glance up at either a green or concrete rooftop for 40 seconds. Those who gazed at the green roof made significantly fewer errors when they resumed the task.

Opal, Forest and Freedom block chosen apps, websites and, when necessary, even the whole internet to help users spend more time on what they want and need to do, rather than reflexively reaching for their phones. In the case of Forest, real-life trees are planted in celebration of time spent away from a phone.

Focus life hacks against digital distractions

1. Swap a smartphone for a flip-phone (don't panic, WhatsApp can be accessed online).

2. Schedule email sessions only twice a day at 9am and 12pm.

3. Swap a Kindle for a paper book – it helps break the digital connection.

Focus time trials

- How long can I work without checking my phone?

- How long can I think without my mind wandering?

- How long can I have a conversation before getting bored?

- How long can I listen to someone before wanting to talk about myself?

- How long can I watch one screen at a time?

- How long can I be incommunicado?

Discover task batching

Much like batch booking, it can be efficient spending a day working solidly on a heap of similar tasks, rather than piecemeal tasks here and there. By allotting time to similar tasks, we leverage the power of focus and reduce the limiting brain freeze that comes with constantly shifting from different types of tasks.

How to task batch

1. List your imminent, important and mundane tasks. These must encompass everything, from mopping the floor or regrouting the bathroom, to filing a tax return or applying for a sports training club.

2. Categorize tasks. Separate out the practical and paperwork-based tasks and batch your tasks into groups that require similar skills.

3. Schedule batch tasks. Work out the time required for the grouped tasks and allocate time on your calendar.

4. Focus and complete. Concentrate only on the allocated batch tasks, don't attempt to multitask and work through the jobs until complete.

Clean your desk

Six reasons why a clean desk helps
your concentration:

1. There are no obvious items, notes,
   rubbish and food to distract.

2. There is no subliminal message
   from the mess telling you you're
   a messy person.

3. You have more space to move, stretch and think.

4. You'll find things more easily.

5. A clean desk helps you feel productive and in control.

6. Cumulatively, you will find that organization comes more naturally.

Meet Vilfredo Pareto, the Italian economist who discovered the Pareto Principle, the idea that around 20 per cent of inputs lead to 80 per cent of outcomes. In terms of focus, the Pareto Principle suggests that 80 per cent of our successes come from 20 per cent of our effort.

Use the Pareto Principle to improve focus

1. Determine which 20% of your tasks contribute to 80% of your work or personal success.

2. Examine which 20% of your habits contribute to 80% of your ability to focus.

3. Eliminate the 20% of apps that cause digital distractions.

When saying NO to someone in order to retain your focus on your chosen task, remember the line: 'Yes to the person – no to the task.'

According to a study by the University of California, every time we are interrupted or interrupt ourselves to check the family WhatsApp or browse Instagram, it takes us 23 minutes and 15 seconds to refocus on what we were supposed to be doing.

Be more air traffic controller

All hail the magnificent air traffic controllers, who have one of the most focus-intense jobs around. Initial training in simulators begins at 20–30 minute intervals only, as high-intensity concentration is built up. Shifts are highly regulated and air traffic controllers can only work for a maximum of 120 minutes per shift. Most shifts are closer to 1–1.5 hours, with 30-minute breaks in between.

During breaks, air traffic controllers are encouraged to do non-work-related activities so that their brains can rest and recharge. The limited amount of time an air traffic controller can work in one shift is a reminder that even the most highly trained experts can manage no more than two hours of pure concentration in one sitting.

Examining whether people can focus on two tasks at the same time, scientists reporting in the *Psychonomic Bulletin & Review* found that only 2.5 per cent of people could drive well and check their phone at the same time, suggesting very clearly that the overwhelming majority of people can only focus optimally on one task at a time.

" If we wait for the moment when everything, absolutely everything is ready, we shall never begin."

IVAN TURGENEV

Book 'Contingency Time' in your daily calendar

An hour at the end of the day, for example. Whenever a thought comes up, like, 'Ooh, I must book that dentist's appointment/order some gold trainers/browse recipes for dinner, etc.' remind yourself that these can be actioned during your 'contingency hour.'

Don't be afraid of using 'Unavailable' on work or family calendars. Resist the urge to apologise, follow the British royal family's dictum of 'never complain, never explain', and allow yourself time apart to tie up loose ends, rattle through a list of jobs or simply recharge.

Use the 'three email rule'

If communication on a subject with family or colleagues takes more than three emails to resolve, call instead. You will find a phone conversation is often more focused than fragmented email chains.

Avoid the intimidation that comes with a whole eight-hour day in which to complete a task by scheduling regular breaks. Chunk out time into manageable segments and use the breaks as rewards for productive focus.

" The secret of getting ahead is getting started. The secret of getting started is breaking your complex overwhelming tasks into small manageable tasks, and starting on the first one."

MARK TWAIN

Have you ever experienced being 'in flow'?

If yes – lucky you. If no, then consider the experience of creatives, makers and those engaged in physical and mental activity that is so absorbing all other aspects of life slip by. Almost in a trance-like state, those in flow later describe a feeling of ecstasy that comes from being fully engaged in an activity. Think of the concert pianist absorbed within the music or the child colouring, deeply involved in their task – there is a brilliant productivity that emerges to the delight of the person at the centre.

How to experience 'being in flow'

1. Understand that this is not just the preserve of artistic types, it's a state of being that anyone can experience when fully absorbed in something they love – think of the downhill skier where the world literally melts away from them.

2. Give yourself permission to fully immerse yourself in your chosen activity. It is hard to be in flow if overly self-conscious.

3. Appreciate that being in flow comes with experience – it's unlikely you will experience the exhilarating flow of an opera singer during your first session at a local choir.

4. Work at your chosen activity – do it regularly, become brilliant at it and allow yourself to be sublimated within the greater experience you are creating.

5. Do not expect an outcome – just enjoy the ride.

" Whether I was in my body or out of my body as I wrote it, I know not. God knows."

GEORGE FRIDERIC HANDEL
on composing the *Messiah* in 24 days

What's the difference between being 'in flow' and 'hyperfocus'?

While 'hyperfocus' and 'being in flow' both involve intense concentration for prolonged periods of time and the ability to tune out external stimuli to the extent that time gallops away, hyperfocus has the possibility of destabilizing a functional daily life. The science around the subject is young but there may be a connection between those with ADHD and an ability to hyperfocus.

How to successfully harness your hyperfocus

1. Use a grid to allocate hyperfocus time. Timetabling space in which to disappear into a task completely makes mundane daily life more manageable.

2. Tell others around you that you may be busy for some time so that they are able to manage their time around your 'absence'.

3. Set time limits and remind yourself to check in on usual daily life – those teeth still need to be cleaned.

If you routinely succumb to brain fog and find yourself unable to focus, it's a good idea to ask for a medications review with your doctor. Some prescriptions for depression and allergies can slow down processing abilities.

Famous acts of focus

Drag yourself away from the comforts of the 21st century to 9th-century England and the company of King Alfred the Great. His fragile kingdom of Wessex is being besieged by Viking invaders who are close to destroying fledgling England. In 878 King Alfred retreats to the Somerset marshland and stumbles across a peasant's cottage. A woman asks if he could watch her cakes while she runs an errand. King Alfred sits in the hovel and thinks deeply about how to save his kingdom.

So focused is the king that he forgets about the cakes, which famously burn. The woman returns to scold this hopeless fellow, not realizing he is the king. Had King Alfred not been able to focus and think at this crucial moment, the history of England would have taken a violently different turn. As it was, he turned things around and lived long enough to teach England to read again (they'd forgotten in the Dark Ages) and invent a candle clock.

Marie Curie, one of history's pioneering scientists, who conducted groundbreaking research into radiation, is a great example of both the positive and negative results of hyperfocus. Often sleeping in her laboratory – which she affectionately called their 'miserable old shed' – Marie and her husband Pierre prioritized their scientific work over everything else.

We all owe a debt of gratitude to this hyperfocused woman who eventually died from an illness thought to have been triggered by constant and high exposure to radiation.

" It became a serious problem how to take care of our little [daughter] Irène and of our home without giving up my scientific work. Such a renunciation would have been very painful to me, and my husband would not even think of it; he used to say that he had got a wife made expressly for him to share all his preoccupations.

Neither of us would contemplate abandoning what was so precious to both... It can be easily understood that there was no place in our life for worldly relations. We saw but a few friends, scientific workers, like ourselves, with whom we talked in our home or in our garden, while I did some sewing for my little girl."

MARIE CURIE

Q: I've always been a daydreamer. Concentration's just not my thing. Will I ever be able to focus?

A: We should all be cautious of using sweeping statements about ourselves. Query such all-encompassing pronouncements – are you really *always* a daydreamer? Jot down times when you have been able to concentrate – there will be many such occasions – and contemplate why you zip through certain events and tasks and not others.

Anyway, daydreaming can be beneficial for focus. A relaxing bout of staring out of the window and pondering the imponderable can rest the brain, boost creativity and help with emotional regulation, allowing for greater focus later.

" Sit in reverie and watch the changing colour of the waves that break upon the idle seashore of the mind."

HENRY WADSWORTH LONGFELLOW

Focus asks of us that we only give what is necessary, only put our energies where they are invited and do not fill space with clattering nonsense.

" Have more than you show, speak less than you know."

WILLIAM SHAKESPEARE

Questions to ask at the centre of the day:

Am I happy with my focus levels?

Are the distractions urgent or can I address them later?

Is the time right to refocus my energies?

German philosopher Immanuel
Kant said that, to be happy, we need
something to do, someone to love and
something to hope for. Are we placing
our focus on the right areas? Are
we orientated towards a worthwhile
project, loving relationships and noble
future hopes?

" Nothing is impossible to a determined woman."

LOUISA MAY ALCOTT

" Far away there in the sunshine are my highest aspirations. I may not reach them, but I can look up and see their beauty, believe in them, and try to follow where they lead."

LOUISA MAY ALCOTT

Always running from one thought to another, putting down one task to begin another, stopping to call someone and then tapping out a message to someone else? Such flighty behaviour is multitasking gone wrong, where nothing settles and thoughts buzz around our brains endlessly, unable to focus.

Neuroscience teaches us that brains need time and space to allow thoughts to consolidate into understanding.

Five brain-training apps to improve cognitive ability and attention spans

CogniFit: Tailored to suit personal needs, these brain games are designed by scientists to improve attention, memory and executive functions.

Elevate: Promises to help learners improve their productivity, earning power and self-confidence in skills like reading, writing, speaking, memory and maths.

Lumosity: Works with 100 researchers from around the world to create games to improve thinking speed, problem-solving ability, memory, flexibility and attention.

Peak: Offers a mix of games and challenges, dedicated to lifelong brain training for cognitive health.

BrainHQ: Focuses on improving visual processing, hearing, attention, memory and problem-solving skills through a series of exercises designed by neuroscientists.

Caution – when reaching for an app on your phone that promises to improve your concentration, perhaps ask yourself if using your phone is really the best way of improving your focus?

What to do instead:

- Read a book.
- Write a letter.
- Nothing – for as long as you dare!

" Right now, a moment of time is passing by... we must become that moment."

PAUL CÉZANNE

One of the reasons phones are so addictive is that they provide stimulation both for our hands and minds. From worry beads and rosaries, to smoking and vaping, we have long enjoyed fiddling with things.

Here are some suggestions of old-school activities that keep our fingers busy and give space for our minds to focus:

- Lego
- Crochet
- Origami
- Knitting
- Puzzles
- Rubix cube
- Cross-stitch
- Whittling

Brain regions involved in developing focus and consolidating understanding:

Hippocampus: vital for forming memories, it encodes and initially stores information.

Prefrontal cortex: works on higher-order cognitive functions, including decision making and problem solving. It interacts with the hippocampus to process and consolidate information. Over time, information is gradually transferred from the hippocampus to the neocortex (outer layer of the brain) for long-term storage.

Amygdala: Plays a role in emotional memory, influencing how memories are stored and retrieved.

All of this brain activity requires good sleep and mental rest.

Did you know that ancient Greek philosopher Socrates thought that writing should not be encouraged for fear it would stop people's ability to use their memory. In some ways it's reassuring to learn that even 2,500 years ago, scholars were worrying about the latest technology and its adverse effects on people's ability to concentrate!

" *If men learn this [writing], it will implant forgetfulness in their souls; they will cease to exercise memory because they rely on that which is written, calling things to remembrance no longer from within themselves, but by means of external marks.*"

SOCRATES

Blessed are those who have experienced the intoxicating feeling of 'being seized by the muse' – the act of being so absorbed in a task or period of creation that it feels as if a divine force has taken possession of your senses. The concept is an ancient one and traces its roots to the ancient Greeks, but the Nine Muses retain their significance today for representing the truth that we are fallible and frail but can become magnificent when correctly focused.

Luis de la Fuente, manager of the Euros 2024-winning Spanish football team, has often repeated the idea that hard work beats talent when talent doesn't work. He embeds this idea with the teams he coaches and inspires the team to repeat 'We are champions' at the start of any tournament. With an ethic to work hard and a will to win, it's easy to understand Spain's footballing triumphs.

Meet the nine ancient Greek muses

Nine sisters and daughters of Zeus and Mnemosyne (memory), the muses are described as long ago as the 8th century BCE by the poet Hesiod as reigning over the Arts and Sciences. They are reminders that we all need ethereal inspiration when attempting to direct our energies.

Calliope – epic poetry

Clio – history

Erato – literature

Euterpe – music

Melpomene – tragedy

Polymnia – song

Terpsichore – dance

Thalia – comedy

Urania – astrology and astronomy

Five-time Olympic medal-winner Tom Daley has competed as an elite diver since the age of 14. Such breathtaking skills require daily focus. In the run up to international competitions, Tom Daley is reported by olympics.com to complete:

11 sessions in the gym a week

11 sessions in the pool

1 session of movement-based exercise such as ballet

6 days training a week

6 hours a day working on weight lifting, cardio, yoga

125kg squat lifts

80kg on his back while doing press-ups

1 day of rest a week. Tom enjoys cooking and knitting in his downtime.

" *In the end, it's extra effort that separates a winner from second place. But winning takes a lot more than that, too. It starts with complete command of the fundamentals. Then it takes desire, determination, discipline and self-sacrifice. And finally, it takes a great deal of love, fairness and respect for your fellow man. Put all these together, and even if you don't win, how can you lose?* "

JESSE OWENS

Be inspired by Jesse Owens, the winner of an unprecedented four gold medals at the 1936 Berlin Olympics, and ask yourself whether you have the necessary focus to succeed at your desired goal.

- Have you got the fundamentals right? Are you eating and sleeping well and properly focused on your loving relationships?

- Have you the necessary determination, discipline and self-sacrifice?

- Are you approaching your goal with an attitude of fairness and respect towards your fellow competitors?

Where shall our focus lie? On our emotions or on our actions? Many of history's greatest minds have all agreed we should put our minds to activities rather than ruminating on our feelings. What do you think?

" Men are all alike in their promises. It is only in their deeds that they differ."

MOLIÈRE

" *Victory awaits him, who has everything in order – luck we call it. Defeat is definitely due for him, who has neglected to take the necessary precautions – bad luck we call it.* "

ROALD AMUNDSEN

" *We look up. For weeks, for months, that is all we have done. Look up. And there it is – the top of Everest. Only it is different now: so near, so close, only a little more than a thousand feet above us. It is no longer just a dream, a high dream in the sky, but a real and solid thing, a thing of rock and snow, that men can climb. We make ready. We will climb it. This time, with God's help, we will climb on to the end.* "

TENZING NORGAY
on reaching the summit of Mount Everest in 1953

Focus asks that we understand the difference between ability and attitude.

Ability: what are we naturally capable of achieving

Motivation: underscores our approach to success

Attitude: how well we will work towards our goal

Mind-blowing episodes of focus in history

Thirty-three when he began painting the Sistine Chapel in 1508, Michelangelo's artistic endeavour is one of the supreme acts of concentration in human history. The Renaissance genius painted iconic scenes from the Book of Genesis onto wet plaster in an act of artistic devotion that took him four years. If he could manage this, surely we can attempt to spend four hours without stopping work to check the sports results?

" *To paint the vast expanse of the Sistine Chapel ceiling, Michelangelo undertook a monumental task that would test the limits of human endurance. Forced into an unnatural and physically demanding position, he spent countless hours lying on his back, arms outstretched, applying the wet plaster with meticulous care.*

The strain on his body was immense, and the unnatural posture led to severe pain and discomfort. His eyes, in particular, suffered greatly from the constant upward gaze, resulting in temporary vision problems. For months afterward, he could only read or examine his designs while looking upwards."

GIORGIO VASARI

Focus inspiration

Pin an image of the Sistine Chapel to
your work station to remind yourself
what can be achieved with a bit of wet
plaster and oodles of concentration.

" I have no secret but hard work. This is a secret that many never learn, and they don't succeed because they don't learn it. Labour is the genius that changes the world from ugliness to beauty, and the great curse to a great blessing."

J.M.W. TURNER

" *To arrive at the simplest truth requires years of contemplation... If I have ever made any valuable discoveries it has been due more to patient attention than any other talent.*"

SIR ISAAC NEWTON

How to cultivate Sir Isaac Newton's 'patient attention'

- Understand that focus does not always need to be work related and carried out in frenzied bursts of absorbed activity.

- Focus can take place over many years of sustained thought concerning a given subject.

- Give yourself permission to mull over ideas for their own sake.

- Don't expect an immediate outcome.

- Think in terms of decades not days.

- Give patient attention to ideas that interest you and wait to see what may or may not happen.

Q: How can we direct our focus to support flourishing happiness?

A: Think of yourself as a young child – a beloved daughter, niece or cousin. What advice would you give them about where to focus their attentions? Are we putting our focus on ourselves in such a way that gives due honour to the person in question? (And if this means focusing less on manicures and more on college work then so be it!)

" But success shall crown my endeavours. Wherefore not? Thus far I have gone, tracking a secure way over the pathless seas: the very stars themselves being witnesses and testimonies of my triumph. Why not still proceed over the untamed yet obedient element? What can stop the determined heart and resolved will of man? "

MARY WOLLSTONECRAFT SHELLEY

We are sometimes guilty of attributing other's success to their innate 'genius' or 'talent' when often their achievements are down to sheer relentless hard work and concentration. Discover how Old Master Michelangelo approached his work:

"*Such was his passion for his art that Michelangelo would often forget about the most basic human needs. He became so engrossed in his work that he neglected to eat or sleep, spending entire days and nights without leaving his studio. His mind was a crucible of ideas, and his hands were tireless in giving form to the visions that consumed him. It was as if the world outside ceased to exist for him, replaced entirely by the beauty and complexity of the artistic world he was creating.*"

GIORGIO VASARI

Is love always the ultimate focus of our emotions? John Keats, the Romantic poet, best conveys the wild absorption that love brings in this letter to Fanny Brawne, his neighbour and fiancée, written in 1819. Keats died of tuberculosis before they could marry.

" *I cannot exist without you – I am forgetful of everything but seeing you again – my Life seems to stop there – I see no further. You have absorb'd me. I have a sensation at the present moment as though I were dissolving... I have been astonished that Men could die Martyrs for religion – I have shudder'd at it – I shudder no more – I could be martyr'd for my Religion – Love is my religion – I could die for that – I could die for you. My creed is Love and you are its only tenet – You have ravish'd me away by a Power I cannot resist.* "

JOHN KEATS

The Ant and the Grasshopper is a harsh but useful fable that reminds us about the importance of focusing on the boring but essential elements of life, not just song and dance, frolics and fun.

" *The ants were spending a fine winter's day drying grain collected in the summertime. A grasshopper, perishing with famine, passed by and earnestly begged for a little food. The ants inquired of him, 'Why did you not treasure up food during the summer?' He replied, 'I had not leisure enough. I passed the days in singing.' They then said in derision: 'If you were foolish enough to sing all the summer, you must dance supperless to bed in the winter.'* "

AESOP

Meet German Romantic painter Caspar David Friedrich, maker of vast canvases of wild nature. In order to so vividly depict storms, forests and mountains, Friedrich would spend days alone in nature focusing on how the trees move, how the smallest blossom emerges, how the mist billows. By allowing himself to become completely absorbed in his subject he was able to convey its brilliance.

" *I must stay alone and know that I am alone to contemplate and feel nature in full; I have to surrender myself to what encircles me, I have to merge with my clouds and rocks in order to be what I am.*"

CASPAR DAVID FRIEDRICH

How to be alone to encourage focus

Have no expectations from these moments of solitude, just let your mind rest – the focus will come naturally later.

1. **Schedule serenity.** Factor in an empty hour somewhere in the day when you can walk out alone, ideally to a place of beauty. Plan nothing.

2. **Leave your phone at home when walking.** Being free of digital distractions is particularly exhilarating when outside in the fresh air – suddenly you find yourself focusing on the birdsong.

3. **Create a sanctuary within the home.** Create a 'Do not disturb' sign and do not be afraid to use it.

Be alive to the happiness that outward focus brings

While we have all been encouraged to self-actualize and work on being 'our best selves', philosophers of all ages have understood that happiness comes from focusing our thoughts and energies on others. Focusing on self-optimization and self-affirmation can be easier than dedicating ourselves to helping others or working out difficult solutions to impractical problems within society, but doing so might just make us happier.

" *Those only are happy who have their minds fixed on some object other than their own happiness; on the happiness of others, on the improvement of mankind, even on some art or pursuit, followed not as a means, but as itself an ideal end. Aiming thus at something else, they find happiness by the way.*"

JOHN STUART MILL

Some of us find it very easy to focus, but alas we concentrate on the wrong things. When planning a holiday or party we focus on everything that could go wrong rather than getting animated about future fun. Such habitual thinking is hard to shift but the first step is noticing a tendency to focus on the negative. After observing this, ask: 'Is it reasonable for me to be dedicating so much of my energy to these ideas?'

" We suffer more in imagination than in reality."

SENECA

Harness the power of memory to expand focus. Learning poems, lyrics, psalms or passages of prose is an effective way of refining concentration. The process of repetition – closing your eyes to absorb the words and listening to each vowel sound to appreciate its meaning – has a powerful impact on your brain's ability to fully take on new information.

How to learn lines/memorize a poem or your favourite song

1. **Speak out the words**, making sure you understand what every word means and why it is where it is in the sentence.

2. **Write out the words.** This forces your mind to see the words and helps transfer them into memory.

3. **Repeat the words** to yourself by covering them up and seeing if you've got them right.

4. **Take a break** to help your mind absorb the words, enjoy a walk or a change of scene.

5. **Use a mnemonic device.** If the poem begins with 'What happens to a dream deferred?' the mnemonic would be WHTADD.

" Memory is the receptacle and sheath of all knowledge."

MARCUS TULLIUS CICERO

" *I think and think for months and years. Ninety-nine times, the conclusion is false. The hundredth time I am right.* **"**

ALBERT EINSTEIN

Are you a painter or a firefighter?

Are you a big-picture thinker able
to focus on one overarching goal or
are you constantly fighting against
small blazes that stop you achieving
your plans? Daily firefighters live in a
constant state of nervous exhaustion
that can be challenging, but not
impossible, to shift.

Next time a blaze begins to distract you from your plans for the day, ask 'Is this fire urgent or important?' If the fire needs your urgent attention, switch your focus to the blaze. If the problem is important, but can be dealt with later, DO NOT give it any immediate focus.

Can you remember those students who would furiously annotate their work with different highlighters and labels? Sometimes for all their apparent concentration they would miss the central point the teacher was making. Don't be deceived by busyness – it is not always a marker of a focused mind.

"A person who is gifted sees the essential point and leaves the rest as surplus."

THOMAS CARLYLE

What to eat to supercharge your
focused mind

**Omega-3 fatty acids to support brain
health and cognitive function:** found in
oily fish such as salmon, mackerel, tuna,
flaxseeds and walnuts.

**Antioxidants to protect brain cells
from damage:** present in berries, dark
chocolate, tea and nuts.

**Vitamin B complex to help convert food
into energy and support brain function:**
found in whole grains, meats and eggs.

**Iron is vital for oxygen transport to the
brain:** iron-rich foods include spinach,
lentils and beef.

Hey – what a great excuse to have a smoked salmon starter and a steak supper, followed by berries in a dark chocolate sauce... I'm just eating this to support my concentration!

" *The first essential for the child's development is concentration. The child who concentrates is immensely happy.*"

MARIA MONTESSORI

" Thinking leads a person to knowledge. They may see and hear, and read and learn, as much as they please; they will never know any of it, except that which they have thought over, that which by thinking they have made the property of his mind. Is it then saying too much if I say, that a person by thinking only becomes truly a human? Take away thought from a person's life, and what remains? "

JOHANN HEINRICH PESTALOZZI

How to cultivate thinking (yes, really!)

'I haven't got time to think...' is a pretty common refrain, but think about it, how often do any of us ever have a good, long think?

Many of us find it impossible to stand in a queue for a coffee without checking our phones; the thought of doing nothing but thinking is anathema. We are used to bustling about being busy, and if not busy, then being entertained by friends, family or our devices. Time alone to just chew the cud is rare. Make space in your daily life for nothing but thinking and see how your ability to focus on tasks improves.

When to do nothing but think

- In the coffee queue

- While walking

- In the bath – try it without a podcast for once

- While cooking – there is no need to check the news while also tossing an omelette

- Waiting for a friend

- On the tube

- Now! Put this book down and think for five minutes

" We do not learn from experience... we learn from reflecting on experience."

JOHN DEWEY

" Put your talent into your work, but your genius into your life."

OSCAR WILDE

Are you focused on action or feeling? Jackie Robinson, the first Black American to play major league baseball, famously said that it didn't matter 'what I believe, only what I do'. This sentiment of action-based focus can help us to move beyond ruminating to activity.

Discover 'box breathing' to immediately refocus from a stressful situation

If this technique is good enough for the US Navy Seals, it's good enough for us. High-pressure life and death situations require a cool mind and an ability to focus intensely on what needs to be done. The Navy Seals famously use the box breathing technique to oxygenate the brain and move from a state of incipient panic to one of calm concentration.

The box breathing technique to rapidly reduce stress and gain high-impact focus

Visualise a square and move along each side as you complete each step. Each of the four basic steps lasts four seconds.

1. **Breathe in**
   Close your eyes, breathe in and slowly count to four.

2. **Hold breath**
   Without firmly clamping your nose or mouth shut, gently hold your breath and count to four.

3. **Breathe out**
   Slowly exhale and count to four.

4. **Hold breath**
   Pause and count to four.

Repeat until your mind is still, your pulse is calm and you feel ready to tackle whatever you have to face.

" Simplify your life. Don't waste the years struggling for things that are unimportant. Don't burden yourself with possessions. Keep your needs and wants simple and enjoy what you have. Don't destroy your peace of mind by looking back, worrying about the past. Live in the present. Simplify!"

HENRY DAVID THOREAU

Sigmund Freud, the Austrian psychologist, wrote that 'All that matters is love and work'. Do you agree? Do you put sufficient focus on these areas? Are there other areas in your life where your focus is concentrated?

Three ways to focus when tired

1. Break up the task into several smaller components.

2. Anticipate it may take longer than it normally would.

3. Begin straight away to ensure an early bedtime!

" *Lose not yourself in a far-off time,
seize the moment that is thine.*"

FRIEDRICH SCHILLER

How to maximize focus if you're an owl

The moon emerges and like a badger you find yourself alert and ready for the night. Leverage your peak productivity hours by creating a focused night-time routine. Remember:

1. You still need 7–9 hours' sleep as an adult, so prioritize consistent sleeping patterns.

2. Expose yourself to natural light during the day, so you can work like a master at night.

3. Use caffeine strategically to boost owl energy.

Questions to ask at the eve of the day

Who did my focus benefit?

How productive was my focus?

By focusing, how do I now feel?

Three reasons why sleep aids focus

1. During sleep, memories are consolidated by the brain without external distractions – think of it as a neural filing system. You wake in the morning refreshed, with a better understanding of what happened the day before and what needs to be done today.

2. Attention, problem solving and decision making are all reinforced by good sleep.

3. Stress is reduced with good sleep, allowing our minds to better regulate unexpected events and challenging decisions.

Sleep well to support focus

There is no silver bullet for good sleep hygiene, just three simple rules:

1. Regular bedtimes – an adult needs between 7–9 hours' sleep a night.

2. No digital devices in bedrooms and avoid using them for at least an hour before sleep.

3. Avoid heavy meals, caffeine and alcohol close to bedtime.

Evening mantras for better focus

I shall embrace sleep as a friend to focus.

Like the night sky, I clear my mind from distractions.

With each drowsy breath I am recharging for a focused tomorrow.

I say goodnight to distractions and welcome tranquillity.

Sleep will bring me renewed mental clarity and focus.

PEOPLE QUOTED

Ada Lovelace, 1815–1852, English mathematician and writer

Aesop, c. 620–564 BCE, Greek fabulist

Albert Einstein, 1879–1955, German-born theoretical physicist

Alexander Graham Bell, 1847–1922, Scottish-born inventor and scientist

Alexander Hamilton, 1757–1804, American statesman and Founding Father

Andrew Carnegie, 1835–1919, Scottish-American industrialist and philanthropist

Caspar David Friedrich, 1774–1840, German Romantic painter

Friedrich Schiller, 1759–1805, German poet, philosopher, historian and playwright

George Frideric Handel, 1685–1759, German-British baroque composer

Giorgio Vasari, 1511–1574, Italian painter, architect, art historian and biographer of Michelangelo

Henry David Thoreau, 1817–1862, American essayist, poet and philosopher

Henry Wadsworth Longfellow, 1807–1882, American poet

Ivan Turgenev, 1818–1883, Russian novelist

J.M.W. Turner, 1775–1851, English Romantic painter

Jesse Owens, 1913–1980, American track and field athlete

Johann Heinrich Pestalozzi, 1746–1827, Swiss educator and social reformer

John Dewey, 1859–1952, American philosopher and educator

John Keats, 1795–1821, English Romantic poet

John Stuart Mill, 1806–1873, English philosopher, economist and politician

Louisa May Alcott, 1832–1888, American author

Marcus Aurelius, 121–180, Roman emperor and Stoic philosopher

Marcus Tullius Cicero, 106–43 BCE, Roman statesman

Maria Montessori, 1870–1952, Italian physician and educator

Marie Curie, 1867–1934, Polish-French physicist and chemist

Mark Twain, 1835–1910, American author and humourist

Mary Wollstonecraft Shelley, 1797–1851, English writer, philosopher and women's rights advocate

Molière, 1622–1673, French playwright and poet

Octavia E. Butler, 1947–2006, American science fiction author

Orison Swett Marden, 1848–1924, American self-help author

Oscar Wilde, 1854–1900, Irish poet and playwright

Paul Cézanne, 1839–1906, French post-impressionist painter

Roald Amundsen, 1872–1928, Norwegian explorer

Rumi, 1207–1273, Persian poet

Samuel Taylor Coleridge, 1772–1834, English Romantic poet and philosopher

Seneca, 4 BCE–65 CE, Roman Stoic philosopher

Sir Isaac Newton, 1643–1727, English physicist and mathematician

Socrates, c. 469–399 BCE, Greek philosopher

Tenzing Norgay, 1914–1986, Nepalese-Indian Sherpa mountaineer

Thomas Carlyle, 1795–1881, Scottish historian, essayist and literary critic

Thomas Huxley, 1825–1895, English biologist and writer

W.E.B. Du Bois, 1868–1963, American sociologist, historian and civil rights activist

William Shakespeare, 1564–1616, English playwright and poet

AUTHOR'S NOTE

As well as compiling Little Books, I work as a
mentor and tutor to children who have been
expelled from school or otherwise refuse to attend.
It is a privilege to be in their company. One
of the trickiest parts of the job is encouraging
students to work at something they do not enjoy
or find difficult – focus initially eludes them. And
yet there are breakthroughs. With goal setting,
concentration time trials and reinforcing the
belief that everyone can work hard at something,
gradually the students learn to focus. I am
thinking now of the 14-year-old boy who believed
he couldn't concentrate and now works at
20-minute stretches, the girl who no longer takes
her phone to bed, sleeps better and was able to
return to school, the 15-year-old who has read
his first book. Even within the most challenging
situations it is possible to reorientate our focus
and work at things we find difficult. I hope some of
the ideas in this Little Book may inspire you too.

USEFUL BOOKS

Feel-Good Productivity: How to Do More of What Matters to You, Ali Abdaal, published by Penguin

Stolen Focus: why you can't pay attention, Johann Hari, published by Bloomsbury

Focus: the hidden driver of excellence, Daniel Goleman, published by Bloomsbury

Concentration: staying focused in times of distraction, Stefan Van Der Stigchel and Danny Guinan, published by MIT Press

USEFUL WEBSITES

verywellmind.com

betterup.com

calm.com

health.harvard.edu

ARTICLES REFERRED TO

'Neural Dynamics of Event Segmentation in Music: Converging Evidence for Dissociable Ventral and Dorsal Networks', Sridharan, D., et al., https://www.sciencedirect.com/science/article/pii/S0896627307005004

'The Cost of Interrrupted Work: More Speed and Stress', Mark, G., et al., https://ics.uci.edu/~gmark/chi08-mark.pdf

'Supertaskers: Profiles in Extraordinary Multitasking Ability', Watson, J. & Strayer, D., https://link.springer.com/article/10.3758/PBR.17.4.479

'Long-term residential sunlight exposure associated with cognitive function among adults residing in Finland', Komulainen, K., et al., https://www.nature.com/articles/s41598-022-25336-6

'Effect of sunlight exposure on cognitive function among depressed and non-depressed participants: a REGARDS cross-sectional study', Kent, S., et al., https://www.ncbi.nlm.nih.gov/pmc/articles/PMC2728098/

'Jumping into the Ice Bath Trend! Mental Health Benefits of Cold Water Immersion', Shetty, M., https://longevity.stanford.edu/lifestyle/2024/05/22/jumping-into-the-ice-bath-trend-mental-health-benefits-of-cold-water-immersion/

'40-second green roof views sustain attention: The role of micro-breaks in attention restoration', Lee, K., et al., https://www.sciencedirect.com/science/article/abs/pii/S0272494415000328?via%3Dihub

'Imagery use in sport: Mediational effects for efficacy', Short, S., et al., https://www.tandfonline.com/doi/abs/10.1080/02640410400023373

Managing Director Sarah Lavelle
Assistant Editor Sofie Shearman
Editorial Assistant Ellie Spence
Words Joanna Gray
Series Designer Emily Lapworth
Designer Alicia House
Head of Production Stephen Lang
Production Controller Martina Georgieva

Quadrille, Penguin Random House UK, One Embassy Gardens, 8 Viaduct Gardens, London SW11 7BW

Quadrille Publishing Limited is part of the Penguin Random House group of companies whose addresses can be found at global. penguinrandomhouse.com

Penguin
Random House
UK

The publisher has made every effort to trace the copyright holders. We apologize in advance for any unintentional omissions and would be pleased to insert the appropriate acknowledgement in any subsequent edition.

Published by Quadrille in 2025

www.penguin.co.uk

A CIP catalogue record for this book is available from the British Library

ISBN 978 1 83783 288 0
10 9 8 7 6 5 4 3 2 1

Printed in China by RR Donnelley Asia Printing Solution Limited

The authorised representative in the EEA is Penguin Random House Ireland, Morrison Chambers, 32 Nassau Street, Dublin D02 YH68.